Two Awesome Fre

I want to say "Thank You" for buying my book so I've put together a few, awesome free gifts for you.

The Essential Kitchen Series Cooking Hacks & Tips Book

&

100 Delicious New Recipes

These gifts are the perfect add-on to this book and I know you'll love them.

So visit the link below to grab them now!

www.GoodLivingPublishing.com/essential-kitchen

Improve Your Memory and Remember Everything

A Guide on How to Develop, Train, and Use Your Memory to Full Capacity and Increase Your Productivity

Table of Contents

Introduction

A strong memory relies on upon the wellbeing and imperativeness of your brain. Whether you're an understudy examining for last test of the years, a working proficient keen on doing everything you can to stay mentally sharp, or a senior hoping to save and upgrade your dim matter as you age, there are heaps of things you can do to improve your memory and mental execution.

They say that you can't instruct an old pooch new traps, however in terms of the brain, researchers have found that this old saying essentially isn't valid. The human brain has a surprising capacity to adjust and change—even into seniority. This capacity is known as neuroplasticity. With the right incitement, your brain can shape new neural pathways, adjust existing associations, and adjust and respond in regularly evolving ways.

The brain's amazing capacity to reshape itself remains constant regarding the matter of learning and memory. You can outfit the characteristic force of neuroplasticity to build your subjective capacities, upgrade your capacity to learn new data, and improve your memory at any age.

When you've come to adulthood, your brain has created a large number of neural pathways that help you process and review data rapidly, take care of commonplace issues, and execute well known errands with at least mental exertion. In any case, if you generally adhere to these well-worn ways, you aren't giving your brain the incitement it needs to continue developing and creating. You need to shake things up every once in a while!

Memory, as strong quality, obliges you to "utilize it or lose it." The more you work out your brain, the better you'll have the capacity to transform and recall data. Be that as it may, not all exercises are equivalent. The best brain activities break your routine and test you to utilize and grow new brain pathways.

Tips to improve your memory

There is no such thing as an "awful memory", and everybody can improve their memory, the length of you are not experiencing memory misfortune as a medicinal condition. If you need to improve your memory, there are various things you can do, from eating blueberries to utilizing a mixed bag of mnemonic devices. If you're hopeful and committed, you'll have the capacity to improve your memory, whether you need to win the World Memory Championships, expert your history test, or essentially recall where you put your keys.

Trying Memory Tricks

1. Say things you need to recall out loud. If you experience difficulty recalling whether you took your medicine each morning, simply say, "I just took my pharmaceutical!" directly after you took it, to fortify this thought in your brain. Saying this out loud will help you recall that you did to be sure take your

prescription. This also lives up to expectations if you're meeting another individual and would prefer not to overlook his name. Simply rehash the name actually after you learn it: "Hello there, Sarah, it's pleasant to meet you." This also attempts to recollect a location or a meeting time. Simply rehash it so anyone might hear to the individual who welcomed you: "The Grand Tavern at 7? That sounds great."

2. Develop your breathing when you need to recollect something. When it's an ideal opportunity to study or recall something new, switch your breathing example to be slower and more profound. More profound and slower breathing really changes the way your brain lives up to expectations, by impelling the brain's electrical heartbeats to change to Theta waves, which regularly happen in your brain in hypnogogic rest.

To initiate your Theta waves, change your breathing to your lower belly - as such, begin breathing profoundly from your stomach. Deliberately moderate your rate of breathing too. After a couple of minutes, you ought to feel more quiet, the Theta waves ought to be streaming in your brain, and you ought to be more open to recollecting new data.

3. Keep in mind a man's name. Utilize a famous trap out of FDR's playbook for retaining a man's name. At the point when a man acquaints themselves with you, picture them with their name composed on their brow. This will relate the picture of that individual with their name.

4. Press an anxiety ball. A few studies recommend that crushing an anxiety ball or making a clench hand with your hand can help you recollect a bit of data later. Before retaining the data, press the anxiety ball in your prevailing hand. For a privilege gave individual, this would be your right hand. When you have to recall the data, press the anxiety ball in your inverse hand for no less than 45 seconds. This basic activity may be sufficient to help you remember.

5. Bite gum. This basic revelation can fortify the brain and improve your obsession, particularly if you have to recall data for 30

minutes or more. Some studies have recommended that visual and sound-related memory improves when a man bites gum by keeping the individual more engaged. When you have to recollect something for under 30 minutes, however, it is entirely not to bite anything.

6. Move your eyes from side to side. Studies reveals that moving your eyes from side to side for only 30 seconds once every day will adjust the two sections of your brain and make your memory work all the more easily. Attempt this trap when you wake up in the morning.

7. Smell rosemary. Studies demonstrate that noticing rosemary can improve your review. Bear a sprig of rosemary or smell rosemary oil once every day. The Ancient Greeks even put a spring of rosemary behind their ears on exam days to help them boost their memories.

Using Mindful Approaches

1. Quit believing that you have a "terrible memory." We all have them - those loathsome recollections that make us have a craving for creeping under the bed to avoid the past. Awful recollections can turn into all-devouring if you don't address the issue head on. Confronting the recollections and portraying them so everyone can hear is a compelling approach to defuse the tension they bring. It may require some investment, however if you're resolved to prevent the recollections from expending your brain, you'll discover a way. Delete those considerations and promise to improve your memory. Commend even little accomplishments to keep yourself encourage.

2. Exercise your brain. Routinely "working out" the brain keeps it developing and goads the advancement of new nerve associations that can help improve memory. By growing new mental aptitudes - particularly complex ones, for example, taking in another dialect or figuring out how to play another musical instrument - and testing your brain with riddles and recreations,

you can keep your brain dynamic and improve its physiological working. Try some fun riddle practices ordinary, for example, crosswords, Sudoku, and different diversions which are sufficiently simple for anybody. Get out of your customary range of familiarity and pick something that is new and testing, which makes you flex your brain muscles. Attempt to play chess or a quick paced table game. A vast part of your brain is initiated when it takes in another aptitude. Adapting new data is also useful, yet since aptitudes require both the admission and yield of data, they practice a bigger bit of your brain.

3. Give yourself an opportunity to enclose a memory. Recollections are extremely delicate in the short-term, and diversions can make you rapidly overlook something as basic as a telephone number. The way to abstain from losing recollections before you can even frame them is to have the capacity to concentrate on the thing to be associated with a while without contemplating different things, so when you're attempting to recall something, maintain a strategic distance from diversions and convoluted assignments for a couple of minutes.

4. Take better pictures. Regularly we overlook things not on account of our memory is awful, but instead on the grounds that our observational abilities need work. One normal circumstance where this happens is meeting new individuals. Frequently we don't generally take in individuals' names at first in light of the fact that we aren't generally focusing on recalling that them. You'll see that if you endeavor to recollect such things, you'll improve.

One approach to prepare yourself to be more attentive is to take a gander at a new photo for a few moments and after that turn the photo over and portray or record the greatest number of points of interest as you can about the photo. Have a go at shutting your eyes and imagining the photograph in your mind. Utilize another photo every time you attempt this activity, and with standard practice you will discover you're ready to recollect more points of interest with significantly shorter looks of the photographs.

5. Include different faculties. You can invigorate more parts of your brain by utilizing whatever number detects as could be expected

under the circumstances when remembering data. At the point when a bigger piece of your brain is dynamic, your capacity to trigger your memory banks will increase.

Write it out. The procedure of composing data by hand invigorates your brain and makes it simpler to recall the data later. Writing is far less compelling, on the other hand. When you do sort out data, utilize aodd textual style. When you complete, read it back. At the point when something is a battle to peruse, you have to focus on it more, which can help fix it into your memory all the more immovably. Rehearse or relate the data. Let yourself know or tell someone else the data. Listening to yourself present the data will include your feeling of hearing. If you have to disclose the data to the next individual so that he or she can comprehend it, also, your memory and comprehension will be improved much further.

6. Use your atmosphere. Change the typical area of things to recollect to do something. If you have to recollect to take your multivitamins each morning, then put the toaster on its side, and

just set it back in its ordinary spot after you've taken your vitamins. Seeing the toaster strange will advise you that something is off and that there's something you have to remember.

If you have to recall something vital, for example, a man's birthday, simply wear your wristwatch on your other wrist. You'll recollect that there was something critical you needed to do when you see that the watch is out of position. The trap is to concentrate on what you need to recall as you adjust the article being utilized. If you are not centered on the bit of data, you will most likely be unable to partner it with the change later on.

7. Use glimmer cards. Blaze cards are particularly helpful for concentrating on. It's basically a card with an inquiry on one side and the answer on the other. Over the span of taking in a point, you would have a pile of cards and would experience them testing yourself. Those that you got right you would put to the other side and survey a couple of days after the fact.

Place the terms you recollected in one heap, and the ones you have to know in another. Continue going until the majority of the cards are in the "know" heap, regardless of the fact that you have to take breaks. Go back to your blaze cards the following day and check whether regardless you've retained the terms on them.

8. Try not to pack for an exam. Packing just attempts to place data in your transient memory. You may recollect the data for your exam the following day, however you will scarcely review the unit when it's an ideal opportunity to take the last. Dividing out your examining is vital on the grounds that it gives your brain time to encode the data and store it in your long haul memory.

Improving Your Lifestyle

1. Compose your life. Keep things that you often need, for example, keys and eyeglasses, in the same place without a doubt. Use an electronic coordinator or every day organizer to stay informed regarding arrangements, due dates for bills, and different undertakings. Keep telephone numbers and locations in

a location book or enter them into your PC or PDA. Improved association can help free up your forces of fixation with the goal that you can recall less normal things. Even if being composed doesn't improve your memory, you'll get a great deal of the same advantages.

2. Choose care as opposed to multitasking. Multitasking may appear like it permits you to finish things speedier, however research recommends that it really causes the brain to ease off by and large. Care permits you to build your center, which improves your memory and rates the brain up. You need around eight seconds of center to submit something to memory. When you multitask, you tend to set data aside quicker than eight seconds, so you're more inclined to overlook it. To rehearse care, all you truly need to do is improve your fixation and invest more energy concentrating on one assignment at once. When you truly need to recall a specific bit of data, spend no less than eight seconds concentrating on that data alone.

3. Practice day by day. Consistent high-impact activity improves course and effectiveness all through the body - including the brain - and can help ward off the memory trouble that accompanies maturing. Practice also makes you more ready and loose, and can in this way improve your memory uptake, permitting you to take better mental "pictures".

Even simply strolling for 30 minutes a day is a fabulous type of activity. Nerve cells discharge neurotropic variables amid activity, and these proteins trigger different chemicals that advance brain wellbeing. Exercise also improves blood stream to the brain, which builds the measure of oxygen your brain gets. Some studies propose that standard activity, whether moderate or overwhelming, can expand the brain's memory focus by maybe a couple percent every year. Without activity, the memory focus will stay stable or may diminish in limit.

4. Decrease stress. Incessant anxiety does truth be told physically harm the brain, it can make recollecting significantly more difficult. After delayed anxiety, the brain will begin to end up

influenced and break down. Anxiety might never be totally killed from one's life, however it most likely can be controlled. Indeed, even impermanent anxieties can make it more difficult to adequately concentrate on ideas and watch things. Unending anxiety can also bring about long haul harm to the hippocampus, which is the place recollections are put away.

Try to unwind, frequently rehearse yoga or other extending activities, and see a specialist if you have extreme endless anxiety as quickly as time permits. Meditate for no less than 15 minutes a day. This will help you ease off your breathing and unwind, and it can improve your core interest. Reduce your caffeine admission. Caffeine can make you feel more restless and pushed. Give yourself a back rub or get one from a companion. This will help your body relax up.

Reduce stress by investing more energy being social with your companions. Being a more social animal and conversing with individuals more will also improve your memory. Anxiety and wretchedness can also make it difficult to focus and recollect data. If you are battling with clinical nervousness or wretchedness issue, you ought to work with your specialist to make sense of an approach to treat these conditions.

5. Silly laugh often. Laughter causes various parts of your brain to light up, and the bits in charge of your memory are among them. Laughing turns out to be significantly more valuable when others are included. A few studies recommend that associating with companions, close relatives, and even pets can moderate your general rate of memory decrease as you age.

6. Eat well and eat right. There are a great deal of home grown supplements available that claim to improve memory, however none have yet been demonstrated to be powerful in clinical tests. A sound eating regimen, be that as it may, adds to a solid brain, and nourishments containing cell reinforcements - broccoli, blueberries, spinach, and berries, for instance - and Omega-3 unsaturated fats seem to advance sound brain functioning.

Feed your brain with so much supplements as Thiamine, Niacin and Vitamin B-6. Some of the proposed sustenance's for your brain are green tea, curry, celery, broccoli, cauliflower, walnuts, crab, chickpeas, red meat, blueberries, and solid fats. Each of these sustenance's contains cancer prevention agents that may ensure your brain and energize the generation of new brain cells. Increase the sum omega-3 unsaturated fat you expend yet diminish omega-6 fats. Omega-3 fats are generally found in salmon and comparable creature sources, while omega-3 fats are commonly found in handled vegetable oils.

You ought to also keep away from sugars and grain starches since these nourishments can contrarily influence your brain. Soaked fats and unhealthy nourishments are correspondingly accepted to thwart your memory, particularly in the long haul. Red wine may improve your memory when expended with some restraint. If you devour more than one glass a day as a lady or two glasses as a man, the liquor can start to debilitate your memory. In little sums, however, the resveratrol flavonoid in wine can expand blood and oxygen stream to the brain. Grape juice, cranberry juice, new berries, and peanuts are said to give a comparable impact. Grazing, or eating 5 or 6 little suppers for the duration of the day rather than 3 extensive dinners, also appears to improve mental limiting so as to work dunks in glucose, which might adversely influence the brain. Verify its sound stuff.

7. Take a stab at expanding your vitamin D admission. Studies propose that low vitamin D may be connected with diminished psychological performance. When vitamin D receptors in your brain are initiated, the nerve development in your brain increments. A percentage of the metabolic pathways for vitamin D are situated in regions of the brain in charge of shaping new recollections. While too much daylight can bring about skin harm, a moderate sum can give all the vitamin D required by the normal grown-up. Vitamin D3 supplements are other option systems for getting satisfactory vitamin D.

8. Rest soundly. Resting improves your neuroplasticity—your brain's capacity to develop—which upgrades the brain's capacity

to control conduct and memory. The measure of rest we get influences the brain's capacity to review as of late learned data. Getting a decent night's rest - at least seven hours a night - may improve you're fleeting memory and long haul social memory, as indicated by late studies led at the Harvard Medical School.

Try to go anyplace from 7 to 10 hours of rest every night. The perfect for most solid grown-ups is eight hours. Go to bed in the meantime and wake up in the meantime consistently. This will make you feel significantly more refreshed. Spend at any rate thirty minutes perusing in informal lodging down before you go to bed. Stopped the TV, you're PC, and some other visual stimulants no less than an hour prior to bed. Take catnaps amid the day. They can help you energize your batteries and support your memory. Your brain also solidifies data into you're long haul memory bank amid rest. If you stay awake, this process won't be able to happen.

Using Mnemonic Devices

1. Use relationship to recollect actualities. A Mnemonic is something which we can use to recollect things much less demanding. As is regularly the case, it could be an expression, a short melody, or something that is effectively recalled, that we use to recollect something that would somehow or another be difficult to recollect. To use affiliation successfully, you can make a picture in your psyche to help you recollect a word or a picture. For instance, if you experience serious difficulties that JFK was the president included in the Bay of Pigs attack, simply picture the good looking president swimming in a sea encompassed by cheerful, oinking pigs. This is completely senseless, however this solid picture in your brain will perpetually help you connect the president with this event.

By making a visual, your brain can focus on a solitary, simple to-identify bit of data. When you review that solitary image, you can also review the bigger strand of data you doled out to it. For instance, as you place your auto keys in your handbag, envision your satchel all of a sudden developing haggles away. Since the picture is such a bizarre one, you're more prone to recollect that it later, which will also help you remind that your auto keys are inside it. The more exceptional or irregular the picture is, the less demanding it will be for your brain to recollect it.

2. Use relationship to recollect numbers. Suppose you continue overlooking your understudy ID each time you have to utilize it once more. Simply separate the number into littler lumps and make pictures connected with those pieces. Suppose the number is 12-7575-23. Figure out how to make these numbers important. Suppose "12" happens to be your home number, "75" happens to be your grandma's age, and the number "23" is Michael Jordan's shirt number. This is what you can imagine to recollect the number:

Picture your home with two duplicates of your grandma remaining to one side, signifying that the house starts things out. At that point envision Michael Jordan remaining to one side of your grandmas. There you have it - 12, 7575 and 23, the b-ball star.

3. Use piecing. Chunking breaks a wide rundown of numbers or different sorts of data into littler, more reasonable pieces.

Breaking so as to recall a 10-digit telephone number it down into three arrangements of numbers: 555-867-5309.

4. Use rhymes and similar sounding word usage. Rhymes, similar sounding word usage, and even jokes are a paramount approach to recall more everyday statistical data points. Utilizing a mixture of regular and senseless rhymes can help you review fundamental data. For instance, if you're attempting to make sense of if April has 30 or 31 days, simply say the old rhyme so anyone might hear: "Thirty days has September, April, June, and November." Then you'll recollect that April does in reality have 30 days. Here are some different rhymes to use as memory tools:

In fourteen-hundred ninety-two, Columbus cruised the sea blue. A kid can take in the letter set by singing it to the tune of Twinkle, Twinkle, and Little Star, which makes the letters rhyme.

5. Use acronyms. Acronyms are another brilliant tool for recalling a mixture of things, from the names of the five Great Lakes to the

words utilized as conjunctions. You can utilize a prominent acronym, or make one for yourself. For instance, if you're setting off to the store and know you just need Butter, Lettuce, Bread, and Uncage, then simply make a word out of the first letter of every term: Knob - Butter, Uncage, Lettuce, and Bread. Here are some prominent acronyms to utilize:

HOMES. This one is utilized for recalling the Great Lakes: Huron, Ontario, Michigan, Erie, and Superior.

ROY G. BIV. This current man's name can help you recall the shades of the rainbow: Red, Orange, Yellow, Green, Blue, Indigo, and Violet.

FOIL. This will help you recall how to increase two binomial terms: First, Outer, Inner, Last.

FANBOYS. This acronym can help you recall straightforward organizing conjunctions: For, And, Nor, But, Or, Yet, So.

6. Use acrostics. Acrostics are like acronyms, with the exception of rather than simply recollecting the acronym, you can recall another sentence made out of the first letters of an arrangement of words that you need to retain in a sure request. For instance, you can say, "My exceptionally enthusiastic mother simply sent us noodles." to take in the request of the planets: Mercury, Venus, Earth, Mars, Jupiter, Saturn, Uranus and Neptune. You can also make up acrostics of your claim. Here are a couple of more prominent acrostics:

Each Good Boy Does Fine. This is utilized for retaining the lines on the treble music staff: EGBDF. Never Eat Sour Watermelons. This is utilized for recollecting the purposes of a compass in clockwise request: North, East, South, and West. Another great sample is Never Eat Shredded Wheat which also rhymes too. Ruler Philip Can Only Find His Green Slippers. Utilize this to remember the request of the classification framework: Kingdom, Phylum, Class,Order, Family, Genus, and Species. If you don't mind Excuse My Dear Aunt Sally. Utilize this to recall the request of operations in science: Parenthesis, Exponents, Multiplication, Division, Addition, and Subtraction.

7. Use the technique for Loci. This technique has been utilized following the season of Ancient Greece. This procedure obliges you to partner things as far as spot or area to help you recollect the full arrangement of data. To utilize this technique, just envision putting the things you need to recall along a course you're exceptionally acquainted with, or in specific areas in a well-known room or building. To start with, pick a natural way; then, picture the things you need to do or remember along that way.

If you expected to retain the acronyms HOMES, FANBOYS, and FOIL, you can picture a little home, on your entryway patio, an uproarious gathering of fan young men giving a shout out to your stairs, and some foil wrapped around your bed. When you sort out a rundown of data by saying, "in any case," "in the second place," et cetera, you are using an essential interpretation of the technique for loci.

Tips to Remember Everything

Memory hardship is a distinctive side effect of maturing, however it begins route before the silver hair and dentures — conceivably when we're as youthful as 20 . A few analysts accuse absent mindedness for our tweeting and Googling, proposing that multitasking and a consistent flood of data may be harming our memory. Different parts of our lifestyle, similar to nap time and working out also assume a key part. Luckily, there are heaps of procedures that may help keep our memory sharp — before we begin rehashing stories that begin with, "When I was your age."

Improve General Memory

Get some rest. Only one night of lack of sleep can harm our short- and long haul memory, and dusk 'til dawn affairs may cut down our capacity to hold new data by 40 percent! That is on account of, amid rest, the brain selects data worth recollecting and reinforces new recollections. What's more, hey you twenty-year-olds, look at this: One study found that lack of sleep has a more adverse impact on individuals in their 20s than on children of post war America. Notwithstanding age, if those prescribed seven to nine hours of rest appear to be inconceivable, an hour long snooze can also improve memory and review.

Move it. As though there aren't sufficient motivations to put on those running shoes, here's another: Exercise can improve memory and learning — regardless of the possibility that it's only 30 minutes of day by day strolling. Researchers think activity helps the extent of the hippocampus, the piece of the brain that procedures new data and assumes a part in long haul memory stockpiling.

Work the psyche. Have a go at using so as to switch things up a non-prevailing hand or taking another course to work. On the other hand begin utilizing the brain as a part of the ways you've been utilizing the telephone, such as remembering telephone numbers and addresses or composing headings on paper as opposed to utilizing a GPS. Need a speedy lift me-up? A decent out some espresso could very well support that memory and also any brain-preparing amusement.

Keep in mind Random Things

Recognize what's in a name. Continue rehashing another name in your mind or utilization it in discussion as much as you can. Or attach the individual's name to something extraordinary about them, as "Dan the Digital Ninja."

Spare the date. Arrangement ahead with Google Calendar updates and Post-It notes. Extra focuses for remembering the date without help: Try the mnemonic system and make a story by utilizing the numbers as a part of the date. Systemize it. Make customs and create propensities, such as leaving keys in the same place consistently. Go through an agenda of all essentials before going out.

Disregard Me Not — the Need-to-Know

We get a staggering measure of data consistently, yet the brain channels out the greater part of it. The stuff we do notification goes to our transient memory, which can hold around seven units of data for 20 to 30 seconds. Anything critical or impactful moves to another piece of the brain for long haul stockpiling, while the rest gets pushed out to make space for new data coming in. More passionate encounters tend to stay with us, as do exercises we rehash frequently, similar to move schedules.

So why do we generally appear to battle to discover those house keys? Maturing is a major component, and a few studies recommend that the steady decrease in memory starts as right on time as age 20. Other examination recommends we're more averse to recollect things now that data is easily available day in and day out on the Internet! Also, mulls over from the previous quite a while are myth-busting the thought that multitasking is proficient or gainful. A few scientists think multitasking really weakens our transient memory and damages our capacity to concentrate on the most vital data in our surroundings.

Regardless of what the wellspring of those memory issues, the uplifting news is we have you secured. Continue perusing for tips on enhancing memory.

Study Smarter

Study when it tallies. In one study, members who got preparing toward the evening performed preferred on tests over the individuals who were prepared in the morning. Investigating what you've realized before quaint little inn in the wake of awakening can also improve maintenance, however Pythagoras definitely realized that a long time back.

Space out. Different studies have found that a memory system called "divided reiteration" can expand maintenance by up to 50 percent. Fundamentally, divided reiteration includes breaking information into littler units and assessing them reliably through the span of a couple of months. It can also help to test yourself on new data rather than just inactively auditing it.

Recount a story. The crazier the story, the more probable we are to recollect that it! Attempt this system with the shopping rundown: If the first word is "apples," picture a crusty fruit-filled treat on the table and using different words on the rundown to inform a story concerning what happened on the trek to the market.

Conclusion

It was once trusted that brain capacity topped among ahead of schedule adulthood and after that gradually declined, prompting omissions in memory and brain haze amid your brilliant years. Presently it's realized that our cutting edge lifestyle assumes a significant part in adding to subjective decrease, which is the reason presentation to poisons, chemicals, less than stellar eating routine, absence of rest, stretch, and a great deal more can really ruin the working of your brain.

The reverse is also applicable in that a solid lifestyle can bolster your brain wellbeing and even urge your brain to develop new neurons, a procedure known as neurogenesis. Your brain's hippocampus, i.e. the memory focus, is particularly ready to develop new cells and it's presently realized that your hippocampus recovers all through your whole lifetime, if you give it the tools to do as such.

These "tools" are principally lifestyle-based, which is sublime news. You needn't bother with an excessive physician recommended solution or any medicinal method at all to support your brain, and your memory. You just must experiment with the accompanying traps to improve your memory.

Two Awesome Free Gifts For You

I want to say "Thank You" for buying my book so I've put together a few, awesome free gifts for you.

The Essential Kitchen Series Cooking Hacks & Tips Book

&

100 Delicious New Recipes

These gifts are the perfect add-on to this book and I know you'll love them.

So visit the link below to grab them now!

www.GoodLivingPublishing.com/essential-kitchen